I KNOW AMERICA

Our National Monuments

Eleanor Ayer

THE MILLBROOK PRESS
Brookfield, Connecticut

Published by The Millbrook Press
2 Old New Milford Road
Brookfield, CT 06804

5 4 3 2 1

Created and produced in association with Blackbirch Graphics.
Series Editor: Bruce S. Glassman

Library of Congress Cataloging-in-Publication Data
Ayer, Eleanor H.
    Our national monuments / Eleanor Ayer—1st ed.
    (I know America)
    Includes bibliographical references and index.
    Summary: Discusses the history, creators, and symbolism of our national
monuments, both constructed and natural.
    ISBN 1-56294-078-3 (lib. bdg.)
    1. National monuments—United States. [1. National monuments.]
I. Title. II. Series.
E159.A94   1992
973—dc20   91-43230
                                                                          CIP
                                                                           AC

Acknowledgments and Photo Credits
Cover: ©Berenholtz/The Stock Market; Back cover, p. 12: National
Park Service; pp. 4, 5, 6, 9, 11, 14, 16, 18, 20: ©Wm. Clark/National
Park Service; pp. 10, 13: Library of Congress Collection; pp. 22, 39:
The National Portrait Gallery, Smithsonian Insitution; pp. 25, 36:
Culver Pictures; p. 26: AP/Wide World Photos; p. 28: ©Fred Mang,
Jr./National Park Service; p. 32: St. Louis Convention & Visitors
Commission; pp. 34, 40, 42, 43: ©Richard Frear/National Park
Service; p. 35 (top): The Bettmann Archive; p. 35 (bottom): Services
Culturels Français; p. 38: ©Diane Kirk/Georgia Tourist Department;
p. 44: North Carolina Department of Tourism.

Photo Research by **Inge King.**

CONTENTS

Introduction   **4**

CHAPTER 1   **Monuments to America's Leaders**   **7**
The Washington Monument   8
The Lincoln Memorial   9
The Jefferson Memorial   11
Mount Rushmore National Memorial   12

CHAPTER 2   **Honoring America's Soldiers**   **15**
The Tomb of the Unknowns   16
Marine Corps Memorial   17
U.S.S. Arizona Memorial   19
The Vietnam Veterans Memorial   20

CHAPTER 3   **Tributes to Outstanding Americans**   **23**
Benjamin Franklin National Memorial   23
Wright Brothers National Memorial   24
George Washington Carver National Monument   25
Martin Luther King, Jr., National Historic Site   25
Eleanor Roosevelt National Historic Site   27

CHAPTER 4   **Remembering America's Heritage**   **29**
Cabrillo National Monument   29
Christopher Columbus   30
Mesa Verde National Park   31
Jefferson National Expansion Memorial   32
Coronado National Memorial   33
Statue of Liberty National Monument   34
Civil Rights Memorial   36
Confederate Memorial Carving   38
Women's Rights National Historic Park   39

CHAPTER 5   **Preserving Special Places in America**   **41**
National Parks and Monuments   41
Historic, Memorial, and Military Sites   42
Waterways and Land Preserves   44

Chronology   **46**
For Further Reading   **46**
Index   **47**

THE MEANING
OF OUR
NATIONAL MONUMENTS

The Lincoln
Memorial, in
Washington, D.C.

When a famous person dies, or an important event happens, people often look for ways to remember. They want to be certain that the person or event will never be forgotten.

After George Washington died, many Americans named schools, streets, cities, even the capital of the United States, after him. Yet they still continued to look for special ways in which to honor the Father of Our Country. What they decided to do was build a monument that would stand as a symbol of the ideals for which George Washington had so bravely fought: freedom and fairness, courage and leadership. Today the Washington Monument is one of the most visited spots in the world.

This book takes a look at many of America's famous monuments—memorials that were built to show pride in our country. You'll read about memorials to the great leaders in United States history, such as Thomas Jefferson and Abraham Lincoln. You'll learn about monuments that honor the country's brave soldiers and famous battlegrounds. You'll meet outstanding Americans, like Benjamin Franklin and Eleanor Roosevelt, who have also been remembered with U.S. monuments. You'll discover memorials to different cultural groups that have helped shape our country. All of these monuments share a common purpose: They were built or restored to honor an important person, place, or event in American history.

But not all famous monuments in America are made by people. Some are natural wonders so beautiful or unique that they have been set aside by the government as special areas to be protected. The best known of these are America's national parks and monuments. All together, there are more than 350 sites in the country that are National Park Service areas. In this book, you'll read about a few of these wonders—such as Death Valley National Monument in southern California—which help Americans to honor our country's special places of natural beauty.

A statue of Thomas Jefferson stands inside the round Jefferson Memorial in Washington, D.C.

5

CHAPTER

MONUMENTS TO AMERICA'S LEADERS

Washington, D.C., is the home of more of America's famous monuments than any other city in the nation. At its center is the National Mall, a large, grassy, tree-lined area that stretches several city blocks from the Capitol to the Washington Monument. Today the Mall includes a large reflecting pool and the Vietnam Veterans Memorial. Back in 1791, when the plans for America's capital city were being made, what is now the Mall was a marshy, swamplike area. The ground was so wet that it was not solid enough to support a heavy stone structure. Because of this, the site for the Washington Monument, the first of the city's great memorials, had to be moved 360 feet east to more solid ground.

★ The Washington Monument was the tallest structure in the world at the time it was built: 555 feet 5 inches.

★ The monument is made of 90,054 tons of marble.

★ The only person to spend the night inside was a lady from Vermont who was locked in "with bats and howling winds" when the guards went home.

★ In 1934, the outside of the monument was scrubbed for the first time with steel brushes, sand, and water. The cleaning took five months and cost $100,000.

The Washington Monument

The Washington Monument is a giant memorial to America's first president, George Washington. This tribute to the Father of Our Country is the tallest masonry (stone) structure in the world. It is made of blocks of stone, rather than being built around a skeleton of steel; no mortar holds the blocks together. Its shape is an obelisk, a tall, four-sided pillar that tapers to a pyramid at the top.

Around the base of the monument fly fifty flags, one for each of the states. To the west, stretching between the Washington Monument and the Lincoln Memorial, is a 200-foot-long, 160-foot-wide reflecting pool in which the image of the monument can be seen. Until recently, visitors could walk up the 897 steps inside the monument. Now, because of the large number of visitors each year, people must travel to the top by elevator.

Work on the obelisk began in 1848, but a lack of money and the Civil War delayed construction for nearly twenty-two years. When work resumed in 1880, the builders discovered that the marble was not the same shade of white as had been used earlier. Today a dark ring about 150 feet up the monument marks the place where later construction began.

The Lincoln Memorial

Staring from the other end of the reflecting pool, back toward the Washington Monument, is the seated marble form of Abraham Lincoln, America's sixteenth president. The sculpture is huge; in fact, if he were

Inside the Lincoln Memorial is a giant statue of America's sixteenth president. The figure sits in a building designed in the ancient Greek style.

9

LOOKING UNDER LINCOLN

If you visit the Lincoln Memorial in the spring or fall, ask for the tour that takes you down inside the base of the monument. Here you can see stalactites and stalagmites, just as in a cave, formed by water that dripped through cracks in the rock onto the limestone. There are even rusty tools there, left by workers who have tried to repair the damage during the past decades.

Daniel Chester French sculpted the statue of Lincoln that sits inside the Lincoln Memorial.

standing, Lincoln would measure twenty-eight feet tall. Around him is a sort of temple, built to look like the famous Parthenon in Greece. Along the walls are thirty-six marble columns, one for each of the states that belonged to the Union by the end of Lincoln's presidency.

In 1867, two years after President Lincoln was shot, Congress began making plans for a monument to him, but work was not started until 1914. The well-known American sculptor Daniel Chester French crafted Lincoln's statue out of Georgia white marble. Carved into the walls are the words of Lincoln's famous Gettysburg Address.

Every year some two million people visit the Lincoln Memorial. Carved in the marble above the seated sculpture of the president are these words:

> In this temple
> as in the hearts of the people
> for whom he saved the union
> the memory of Abraham Lincoln
> is enshrined forever

The Jefferson Memorial

If you look out the north window from the top of the Washington Monument, you will see the White House, home of the president. From the monument's east window is a view of the Capitol. To the west is the Lincoln Memorial, and to the south is the Jefferson Memorial. They form four ends of a giant cross, with the Washington Monument in the center.

The southern point of the cross, the Jefferson Memorial, honors Thomas Jefferson, third president of the United States and author of the Declaration of Independence. It's easy to spot the Jefferson Memorial because of its dome-shaped roof. Designers patterned it after Jefferson's beloved Virginia home, Monticello, the building pictured on the back of a nickel.

THE WASHINGTON CHERRY BLOSSOMS

The Jefferson Memorial sits on a little piece of land surrounded by the waters of the Tidal Basin. For nearly ten days in April, the 650 cherry trees around the edge of the Tidal Basin bloom with gorgeous pink and white blossoms.

These trees are among the thousands that have been sent as gifts to Americans from the Japanese people since 1912. They are the focus of the famous Cherry Blossom Festival held in Washington each spring.

The Jefferson Memorial

Inside the white marble memorial, on a base of black Minnesota granite, stands a nineteen-foot-high statue of Thomas Jefferson carved by Rudulph Evans. Near the entrance is a group of carvings showing Jefferson and other famous patriots. Words from Jefferson's speeches and writings are carved into four marble panels on the walls. The memorial was started in 1938 and was dedicated five years later, on April 13, 1943, Jefferson's two hundredth birthday.

Mount Rushmore National Memorial

Presidents Washington, Lincoln, Jefferson, and Theodore Roosevelt are remembered in a stone memorial of another kind at Mount Rushmore, South

FACTS ABOUT MOUNT RUSHMORE

★ From the chin to the crown of the head, each Mount Rushmore face is sixty feet high.

★ Noses are twenty feet long, eyes are eleven feet across, and mouths are more than eighteen feet wide.

★ If their bodies too had been sculpted, each statue would be higher than the Washington Monument.

★ The memorial's sculptor, Gutzon Borglum, also worked on the Confederate Memorial Carving at Stone Mountain, Georgia.

★ Work began on the monument in 1927, but because of lack of money, it took fourteen years to finish. During this time, Gutzon died. His son, Lincoln, who had worked on the project with him, completed it.

Dakota. There, on the granite face of a 5,725-foot mountain, giant images of the presidents have been sculpted into the white rock.

The Mount Rushmore figures are in relief, which means they stand out from a flat background. To form the faces, a total of more than 450,000 tons of rock had to be removed from the mountain. The crew used dynamite, blasting to within three or four inches of the working surface and then drilling stubborn spots with jackhammers. For doing the finer finish work, they hung over the edge of the mountain in thick leather harnesses and drilled holes about three inches apart all over the exposed area. When this final layer was chipped away, they smoothed over the entire surface with an air hammer.

C H A P T E R

2

HONORING
AMERICA'S SOLDIERS

In all the wars fought by the United States, more than a million American soldiers have died. We remember them in thousands of monuments across the country, some in small villages, others in large national historic parks. At Valley Forge in Pennsylvania is a memorial to the ragged, starving Revolutionary War soldiers who trained there under General George Washington in the winter of 1777–1778. Shiloh National Military Park in Tennessee—the scene of perhaps the bloodiest battle of the Civil War—has monuments to both Union and Confederate soldiers.

Some 200,000 of the soldiers who have been killed in America's wars, or members of their families, are buried at Arlington National Cemetery in Virginia. Arlington is not the country's only or largest military cemetery, but it is the most famous.

Opposite:
The Vietnam Veterans Memorial in Washington, D.C., honors those who died in the Vietnam War.

The Tomb of the Unknowns

The best known of all the graves at Arlington is one that has no name carved in the marble above it. No one knows who is buried here, and so it is called The Tomb of the Unknowns. Marking the spot where the bodies of four American soldiers lie is a large marble sarcophagus, a tomb-shaped monument. On the sarcophagus are carved the words:

> Here Rests in Honored Glory an American Soldier Known But to God.

The Tomb of the Unknowns is one of America's most symbolic sites. The four bodies buried here—unknown soldiers from World War I, World War II, the Korean War, and the Vietnam War—are symbols of the million-plus American soldiers who have bravely given their lives for the United States.

The Tomb of the Unknowns in Virginia's Arlington National Cemetery honors soldiers from World War I, World War II, the Korean War, and the Vietnam War.

GUARDING THE TOMB OF THE UNKNOWNS

★ Guard soldiers are chosen from a special army unit popularly called "The Old Guard."

★ Guard soldiers must weigh 145 to 200 pounds, stand between five feet eleven inches and six feet two inches tall, be in excellent physical shape, and have a perfect record of behavior and self-control.

★ Guards are trained to march 128 steps per minute in front of the tomb.

★ The guards must look straight ahead at all times. They may not speak, smile, wipe their face, react to the onlookers, or make any move other than to perform their duty.

So special and important is this site that soldiers guard it twenty-four hours a day, regardless of weather. Once an hour during the day, and every two hours at night, the guard changes in a special military ceremony. Many of the four million visitors to Arlington National Cemetery each year come to see the changing of the guard at the Tomb of the Unknowns.

Marine Corps Memorial

Also in Arlington, Virginia, but outside the cemetery, is a statue honoring all United States Marines killed in battle. The memorial—the largest cast bronze statue in the world—is the Iwo Jima Statue. The figures of five marines and a navy medical corpsman are shown plunging an American flag into the rocky summit of Mount Suribachi. The mountain, an extinct volcano on the island of Iwo Jima in the Pacific Ocean, was

The Marine Corps Memorial in Arlington, Virginia, honors all United States Marines that have been killed in battle. The cast metal statue shows Marines raising the American flag on Iwo Jima during World War II.

the scene of fierce fighting during World War II. Here, some 6,800 American marines died and more than 18,000 were wounded.

Joe Rosenthal, a photographer for the Associated Press, took a posed picture of the flag-raising on Iwo Jima. His photograph became as famous as the battle itself. It ran in *Life* magazine and over the years has been featured in paintings, postage stamps, and in dozens of other popular patriotic scenes. From the photo, sculptor Felix de Weldon cast the seventy-five-foot-high Marine Corps Memorial. On November 19, 1954, the monument was dedicated.

Three of the six men who had raised the flag on Iwo Jima were present at the memorial's dedication.

The others were killed in island fighting after the flag was raised. One of the attending survivors was Corporal Ira Hayes, a Native American from Arizona's Gila River Reservation. When Hayes died, his friends brought his body to Virginia and buried it in Arlington National Cemetery, not far from the United States Marine Corps Memorial in which he was depicted.

U.S.S. Arizona Memorial

The event that brought the United States into World War II is remembered in a national memorial at Pearl Harbor, Hawaii. On December 7, 1941, shortly before 8:00 a.m., Japanese warplanes made a surprise attack on the American naval fleet that was docked in Pearl Harbor.

At 8:10 a.m., the battleship *U.S.S. Arizona* was hit by a bomb weighing nearly one ton. Nine minutes later it had sunk, taking more than a thousand navy and marine crew members to their deaths. Two more ships were sunk and several others damaged, and 2,403 Americans were killed at Pearl Harbor that day.

A 184-foot concrete building today spans the sunken battleship and the mass grave of the *Arizona* crew. Boats shuttle travelers from the visitor center on the island out to the *Arizona* memorial. Rising from the broken mast of the sunken battleship is a flagpole. Each day, by order of the navy and in memory of the lost crew of the *Arizona*, the American flag flies from this pole.

The Vietnam Veterans Memorial

The men and women who died in America's longest and most unpopular war are remembered in a unique monument on the Mall in Washington, D.C. The memorial is a wall of black granite, which seems to rise gradually in height, then sink back toward the earth as visitors walk alongside it. On the wall are the names of the 58,156 Americans who died in the Vietnam War (1960–1975).

The memorial was the idea of Jan Scruggs, a veteran who had seen more than half his company killed or wounded in Vietnam. Scruggs wanted the monument to be a tribute to the men and women who had died—not to the war itself.

The black granite wall of the Vietnam Veterans Memorial has 58,156 names engraved on it. These are the men and women who died in America's longest war.

FACTS ABOUT THE VIETNAM VETERANS MEMORIAL

★ Names on the memorial are listed chronologically—in the order in which they were killed.

★ To help visitors find a particular name, the memorial has directories arranged in alphabetical order, giving the location of the name on the granite panels.

★ The black granite came from India and was shipped to Barre, Vermont, to be cut and formed. At Memphis, Tennessee, the names were "grit" blasted into the rock, a process that took five months.

★ At the entrance to the memorial is a life-size bronze sculpture of three Vietnam servicemen. Beside it, a large American flag flies from a sixty-foot pole.

The question of what the memorial should look like was eventually settled by a design contest. The winner was a twenty-one-year-old college student, Maya Lin. "I . . . knew I wanted something horizontal that took you in, that made you feel safe within the park, yet at the same time reminding you of the dead. So I just imagined opening up the earth," said Maya.

On Veterans' Day 1982, the memorial was dedicated. During the ceremony, which lasted five days, the names of all dead and missing Vietnam veterans were read aloud; the reading took sixty hours. Since then, nearly 50 million Americans have visited the Vietnam Veterans Memorial. "A memorial," says designer Maya Lin, "shouldn't tell you what to think, but it should make you think . . . This memorial is for those who have died, and for us to remember."

3

TRIBUTES TO
OUTSTANDING AMERICANS

Benjamin Franklin National Memorial

Many people say that Benjamin Franklin was
America's greatest citizen. Franklin was a leader in
many different areas. He may be best known for his
experiment with the kite, which proved that lightning
is electricity. But he was also a brilliant inventor, a
philosopher, a statesman and representative for the
young American government, an author, a printer, and
a publisher.

As a thank-you to Benjamin Franklin, a national
memorial now stands at his home in Philadelphia,
Pennsylvania. In an eight-sided hall, under a domed
ceiling, is a seated white marble statue of Franklin.

Opposite:
**Benjamin Franklin is
one of America's
most accomplished
Americans. He was
an important force
behind the creation
of the Declaration
of Independence
and the United
States Constitution.**

The Benjamin Franklin National Memorial is part of Independence National Historical Park. This park has often been called "the most historic square mile in America."

Independence National Historical Park has many other important historical sites to see. The two most famous sites are Independence Hall and the Liberty Bell. Independence Hall is where the Declaration of Independence was adopted. The Constitution of the United States was also written there.

The Liberty Bell, which announced America's independence in 1776, sits in a special glass pavilion, a small building across from Independence Hall.

Wright Brothers National Memorial

Two brothers who made the first successful airplane flight are remembered in a monument near Kitty Hawk, North Carolina. On December 17, 1903, Wilbur and Orville Wright made four flights, the longest lasting fifty-nine seconds.

In memory of that historic date and these outstanding Americans, there stands today a sixty-foot-high granite monument at Kill Devil Hills, just down the road from Kitty Hawk. This is where the Wright brothers made many of their early test flights in gliders. The actual takeoff spot for the first December 17 flight is marked by a granite boulder. That flight lasted twelve seconds; the aircraft touched down 120 feet from the takeoff point.

George Washington Carver
National Monument

One of America's most famous scientists, George Washington Carver, began life as a slave on a farm in Missouri. After outlaws kidnapped his mother, young George was raised by the Carvers, the white family who owned him. Even after the Civil War freed him along with the other slaves, young George stayed with the Carvers. He soon developed an interest in plants, and people called him "the plant doctor." George left home to study botany, and for fifteen years traveled the country, working and learning.

When his education was completed, the botanist went to work at Tuskegee Institute, a university in Alabama started by another famous black American, Booker T. Washington. One of Carver's goals was to study farming. He wanted to help his own people learn to raise crops other than cotton, so that they could make better use of their land. His discoveries include three hundred different uses for peanuts and one hundred new ways to use sweet potatoes.

George Washington Carver spent his life studying plants and ways to improve the growing of crops.

Martin Luther King, Jr., National Historic Site

Another one of America's great black leaders is forever remembered at a memorial center in his hometown of Atlanta, Georgia. This was the birthplace, in 1929, of the famous civil rights leader, Martin Luther King, Jr. Dr. King's dream was for people to work peacefully together to bring about changes in our social system—

Dr. Martin Luther King, Jr. led the fight for civil rights in America during the 1960s.

the way we get along with each other. "I have a dream," King said in a 1963 speech, "that my four little children will one day live in a nation where they will not be judged by the color of their skin, but by the content of their character."

Today, the Martin Luther King, Jr., Center for Nonviolent Social Change is working to make that dream come true. The Atlanta center was set up in 1968, the year Dr. King was murdered, and is now run by his widow, Coretta Scott King.

THE MARTIN LUTHER KING CENTER

The following things are part of the Martin Luther King Center:

★ The Center is King's birthplace and boyhood home, where he lived until 1941.

★ The Martin Luther King, Jr., Center for Nonviolent Social Change, working toward Dr. King's dream of equality for all.

★ The Ebenezer Baptist Church, where members of the King family served as pastors for more than eighty years.

★ Dr. King's grave. His body was moved there in the early 1970s to be nearer the places that were so important in his life.

★ The home of Charles L. Harper, the principal of Atlanta's first black public high school.

Eleanor Roosevelt National Historic Site

One of the best-known supporters of human rights was First Lady Eleanor Roosevelt. Although she was the wife of President Franklin D. Roosevelt, Eleanor Roosevelt had a busy career of her own. Mrs. Roosevelt believed strongly in equal rights for all people. She was a leader in the Democratic party, a representative to the United Nations—the world's peace-keeping organization—and a leader of national programs to help the poor. After her husband died in 1945, Mrs. Roosevelt was appointed to the U.S. delegation of the United Nations. As chairperson of the Commission on Human Rights, she became an important force in drafting the U.N. Declaration of Human Rights.

To honor Eleanor Roosevelt, one of her homes has been made a national historic site. Stone Cottage was Mrs. Roosevelt's vacation spot on Val-Kill Creek in Hyde Park, New York. This hideaway, where she took breaks from her busy schedule, was actually a gift from her husband, Franklin. In 1925, he had a stone cottage built for Eleanor and two of her friends. About a year later, a furniture company was hired to build two more buildings at Val-Kill.

Today one of those buildings, Val-Kill Cottage, along with Mrs. Roosevelt's home, make up the memorial to the "First Lady of the World." Many of the furnishings from her home, including some pieces of Val-Kill furniture, are on display. Nearby in Hyde Park is her husband's birthplace. It, too, has been made a national historic site.

CHAPTER

REMEMBERING AMERICA'S HERITAGE

People from many different nations have helped America to grow. These individuals, along with their unique achievements, are remembered in national monuments and memorials.

Cabrillo National Monument

What's your guess? Which national monument gets the most visitors per year—Cabrillo, near San Diego, or the Statue of Liberty? If you answered the Statue of Liberty, you're wrong!

Juan Rodríguez Cabrillo, the explorer for whom Cabrillo National Monument was built, was the first European to visit California. Cabrillo visited there for the first time on September 28, 1542, when he sailed

29

Italian navigator Christopher Columbus sailed unknown seas in 1492. His brave explorations led to the settlement of the New World.

into San Diego Bay. During that trip, he and his crew explored the entire coast of California, claiming it for Spain and Mexico. Today at the monument stands a huge stone statue of Cabrillo, dressed in a Spanish conquistador's suit of armor, with a sword.

One reason why this monument gets so many visitors may have nothing to do with Cabrillo. Each year, thousands of gray whales pass by here on their way to mate in the warmer waters south of California. Cabrillo National Monument, on the tip of Point Loma, is one of the best places to watch them.

Christopher Columbus

Just fifty years before Cabrillo discovered California, an Italian explorer, Christopher Columbus, ventured across the Atlantic Ocean with a fleet of three ships: The *Niña, Pinta,* and the *Santa Maria.* On August 3, 1492, Columbus and his men set sail from Spain. He wanted to prove that by sailing west from Europe, he could find a faster route to the spice- and silk-rich countries of India and China.

In memory of him, a statue stands today in the largest city in the world to bear his name: Columbus, Ohio. To mark the five-hundredth anniversary of the explorer's historic voyage, The Christopher Columbus Quincentennial Jubilee Commission planned a grand year-long celebration in the city in 1992. Highlighting the event was the christening of a full-scale replica of Columbus's flagship, the *Santa Maria.*

Mesa Verde National Park

More than two thousand years ago, Anasazi Indians lived in what is today southwestern Colorado. During the next 1,300 years—long before Europeans came to what is now America—these people would build fantastic apartment-type dwellings under the edges of cliffs in part of the American Southwest.

Although the Anasazi people had no written language, they made pictures on the cliff walls that tell us about their lives. They farmed the land without the help of metal tools. They wove baskets that were tight enough to hold water. From the clay in the soil of the Southwest, they made pottery with beautiful designs.

At Mesa Verde are the remains of some of the great Anasazi cliff dwellings. To preserve these ruins, Mesa Verde has been set aside as a national park. This is only one of many memorials to America's early dwellers. Other ruins are preserved in New Mexico, Arizona, and Utah, where the Anasazi also lived.

FACTS ABOUT MESA VERDE NATIONAL PARK

★ Mesa Verde is the home of the best-preserved collection of cliff dwellings in the United States.

★ The largest dwelling, Cliff Palace, had 217 rooms and was home to 350 people—all under one roof!

★ There are more than four thousand prehistoric sites within the park.

★ Among the ruins are fifty-seven tall stone towers, but historians do not know why they were built.

Jefferson National Expansion Memorial

To honor the thousands of Americans who left their homes in the east to settle the Great American West, a monument stands today on the grounds of the Jefferson National Expansion Memorial in St. Louis, Missouri. This was the jumping-off point in the 1800s for the westward movement, where people gathered from all over the east to join wagon trains.

The monument to these pioneers is the 630-foot Gateway Arch, symbol of the gateway to the western United States. It stands at the center of a beautiful park, named for Thomas Jefferson, the president who made the Louisiana Purchase, which opened the West to settlement. The famous architect and designer Eero Saarinen designed the giant arch.

Across from the park but also part of the national memorial grounds is the Old Courthouse, a building with a huge domed roof like the capitol. It was here, in the early 1860s, that the black slave Dred Scott sued to win his freedom just before the Civil War.

The 630-foot Gateway Arch in St. Louis, Missouri, is a monument to the settlement of America's West by the pioneers in the 1800s.

FACTS ABOUT THE GATEWAY ARCH

★ The Gateway Arch is the nation's tallest monument—taller than the Washington monument.

★ A narrow room at the top has sixteen windows giving a view of the Mississippi River and the land around for up to thirty miles.

★ The Arch has no skeleton; the angle of its legs and the curve of the arc make it stand solidly.

★ The Arch's outer "skin" is stainless steel and weighs 886 tons. The inner "skin" is made of carbon steel.

★ Construction began on February 12, 1963. On October 28, 1965, jacks pushed the two tall legs apart at the top to fit in the last section of the Arch.

★ Even in 150-mile-per-hour winds, the Arch will sway only eighteen inches at the top.

Coronado National Memorial

The Pueblo Indians were peaceful people who farmed the dry southwestern land and got along well with their neighbors. But beginning in 1540, the Pueblos' way of life changed forever. That was the year the Spanish explorer Francisco Vásquez de Coronado arrived in what is now the American Southwest. He was looking for wealth in the Seven Cities of Cíbola. What he found instead were Indian villages.

Coronado's explorations are remembered at a memorial that bears his name. Coronado National Memorial is in the Huachuca Mountains on the Arizona-Mexico border. It is part of a large tract of land that is set aside for natural recreation. It honors not only Coronado, but also the contributions that other Spanish people have made to America.

33

Statue of Liberty National Monument

One of the most famous monuments in America stands at another gateway, to welcome newcomers to our land. Rising proudly from Liberty Island in New York Harbor is the Statue of Liberty, symbol of freedom for people around the world.

With the huge torch held high in her right hand, Lady Liberty is supposed to light the way to freedom for all people. The statue was a gift from France to

The Statue of Liberty stands in New York Harbor and welcomes people from all lands to America.

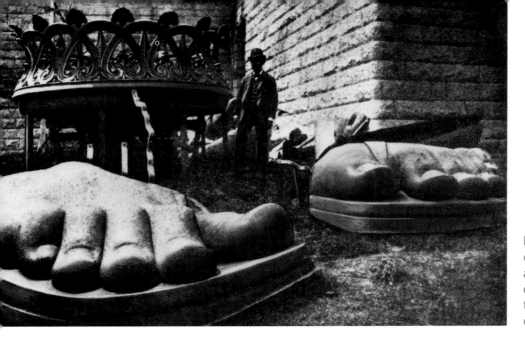

Liberty's giant copper toes sit with a piece of the torch during assembly of the statue in the early 1880s.

America on its hundredth birthday, in 1876. In that year, construction was started, but it was another ten years until the statue was complete.

Visitors to the Statue of Liberty can take an elevator to a deck that looks out over New York City and the harbor. Those with sturdy legs can climb a spiral staircase to the lady's crown, but it is no longer possible to climb into the torch. In the base of the statue is the American Museum of Immigration, which tells the story of the millions of immigrants from around the world who have made America their home.

Also part of this national monument is the former immigration station on nearby Ellis Island. This facility was the entry point for the 12 million immigrants who came to New York from 1892 to 1954. Recently the buildings at Ellis Island have been remodeled and made into a museum that features exhibits on American immigration.

French sculptor Frédéric Auguste Bartholdi designed the Statue of Liberty.

FACTS ABOUT THE STATUE OF LIBERTY

★ The climb to the statue's crown is 354 steps—about the same as walking up a twenty-two story building.

★ The base on which the statue stands cost more to build than the statue itself.

★ The statue itself is 151 feet tall and weighs 225 tons. When measured from the base to the tip of the torch, it's 305 feet.

★ Lady Liberty's index finger is eight feet long.

★ The famous poem by Emma Lazarus that includes the lines, "Give me your tired, your poor, your huddled masses . . . ," was written about the Statue of Liberty and is on a wall inside the base.

★ The sculptor was Frédéric Auguste Bartholdi. The man who designed the base was Alexandre Gustave Eiffel, who would later design the Eiffel Tower in France.

★ The statue was not originally green. Made out of copper, it has turned that color due to exposure to the weather.

Emma Lazarus

Civil Rights Memorial

"It is a place to remember the civil rights movement, to honor those killed during the struggle, to appreciate how far the country has come in its quest for equality, and to consider how far it has to go . . . ." These are the words of the Civil Rights Memorial's designer, Maya Lin. Like the Vietnam Veterans Memorial in Washington, D.C., which she also designed, the Civil

Rights Memorial is made of black granite and lists the names of those killed in the civil rights movement in the 1950s and 1960s.

Since our country began, black people—particularly in the southern states—have been treated unfairly. Black children could not go to the same schools as whites. Blacks had to ride in the backs of buses, and use different public restrooms from those used by white people. Beginning in the 1950s, many people spoke out against this unfairness. It was the beginning of the civil rights movement in America.

In 1989, the Civil Rights Memorial was built by the Southern Poverty Law Center in Montgomery, Alabama. Its purpose is to remember the civil rights movement and to educate people about it.

A MEMORIAL TO CIVIL RIGHTS

On a large granite table at the memorial are listed the names of forty people who were killed in the movement between 1954 and 1968. The following are some of the names:

Virgil Lamar War, 13—Shot by white teenagers in Birmingham, Alabama, while riding on the handlebars of his brother's bicycle in 1963.

Addie Mae Collins, Denise McNair, Carole Robertson, and *Cynthia Wesley*—Four schoolgirls killed when a bomb exploded at the Sixteenth Street Baptist Church in Birmingham in 1963.

Emmett Louis Till, 14—Chicago boy on vacation in Money, Mississippi. Taken from his bed and shot, and his body dumped in the Tallahatchie River.

Samuel Leamon Younge, Jr.—Student shot by a white gas station attendant after an argument over using a public restroom.

Confederate Memorial Carving

Georgia's Stone Mountain Park, sixteen miles east of Atlanta, might be called the Mount Rushmore of the South. The memorial carving, cut into the side of this dome-shaped hulk of rock, honors the leaders of the Confederacy during the Civil War. Seated on their horses are the figures of Jefferson Davis, president of the Confederacy, and two famous southern generals, Robert E. Lee and Stonewall Jackson.

Three sculptors worked on the memorial. The first of them was Gutzon Borglum, who would later carve the Mount Rushmore figures. Work began in 1923, but by 1928, when the memorial was supposed to be finished, only Lee's head was complete. There was no more money. For years, groups tried to raise

FACTS ABOUT THE CONFEDERATE MEMORIAL

★ It is the world's largest piece of sculpture.

★ It is carved on the side of the world's biggest exposed mass of granite.

★ The deepest point in the carving is at Lee's elbow, which stands 11½ feet out from the mountain's surface.

★ Workers could easily stand on a horse's ear or step into its mouth to get out of the rain.

★ The man who completed the carving, Roy Faulkner, had no experience with art; he never had an art lesson or sculpted anything before in his life.

the funds, but no work was done on the project until 1964. In 1970, the memorial was dedicated, with final touches added in 1972.

Women's Rights National Historic Park

Martin Luther King's dream of judging people by "the content of their character" has also been a dream for American women. For nearly 150 years, women in the United States did not have all the rights of men. They couldn't vote; in some places, married women couldn't own property; there were places where girls couldn't even go to school.

By the middle 1800s, women began taking action. In 1848, Elizabeth Cady Stanton and another women's rights leader, Lucretia Mott, met in the town of Seneca Falls, New York. There, they planned a convention that would bring the idea of equal rights for women to the attention of the country. More than three hundred people—men and women—came to the convention. This was the beginning of the modern Women's Movement in America.

Today Seneca Falls is often called the birthplace of women's rights. The homes and offices of Mrs. Stanton and two other women's rights leaders, Amelia Jenks Bloomer and Mary Ann McClintock, are located here. The Wesleyan Methodist Chapel, where the first women's rights convention was held, is another part of the park. Seneca Falls is also home of the National Women's Hall of Fame.

Lucretia Mott was one of America's first leaders in the fight for women's equality. She worked with Elizabeth Cady Stanton in 1848 to organize the country's first convention for women's rights.

C H A P T E R

5

PRESERVING SPECIAL PLACES IN AMERICA

Wouldn't it be too bad if there were gas stations and fast-food restaurants along the rim of the Grand Canyon? What if George Washington's residence at Mount Vernon, Virginia, had been torn down and paved over for a parking lot? Fortunately, the National Park Service protects America's special places so that things like that don't happen.

National Parks and Monuments

The National Park Service is part of the United States government. Under its care are 358 special places in America. The best known of these places are the fifty national parks, among them Yosemite in California,

Opposite:
The Grand Canyon in Arizona is one of America's largest and most dramatic national parks.

Death Valley National Monument has the lowest point in the Western Hemisphere.

Great Smoky Mountains in Tennessee, and the Grand Canyon in Arizona. America's first national park was created on March 1, 1872, when Yellowstone—home of the famous Old Faithful geyser in Wyoming—also became the *world's* first national park.

The park service also takes care of smaller areas called *national monuments.* There are seventy-eight in the United States. One of the most interesting is Death Valley National Monument in California, a desert surrounded by high mountains. The lowest point in the Western Hemisphere is in Death Valley.

Historic, Memorial, and Military Sites

National historic sites are places that are important in America's history. There are sixty-nine of them, many of which are homes of famous people such as former president John F. Kennedy. Another, Chaco Culture National Historical Park in New Mexico, preserves prehistoric Indian ruins.

DID YOU KNOW THAT . . . ?

★ Everglades National Park in Florida is the largest subtropical wilderness (warm, wet region near the tropics) in the United States.

★ America's highest mountain, Mount McKinley (20,320 feet), is in Denali National Park and Preserve in Alaska.

★ Devils Tower, the 865-foot column of rock in northeastern Wyoming, was America's first national monument, and was also a setting for the popular movie about aliens, *Close Encounters of the Third Kind.*

★ Some of the cacti in Arizona's Saguaro National Monument stand fifty feet tall.

★ Eight historic sites from the Revolutionary War days make up the Boston National Historical Park in Massachusetts. Among them are the famous battleship *U.S.S. Constitution*—fondly called "Old Ironsides"; Old South Meeting House, where the Boston Tea Party began; Old North Church, where lanterns were hung to signal Paul Revere before his famous midnight ride to warn colonists of the approaching British troops.

★ The place where Francis Scott Key was inspired to write our national anthem, *The Star-Spangled Banner,* is now a national monument and historic shrine: Fort McHenry in Maryland. It was during the bombardment of the fort by the British in the War of 1812 that Key began his famous poem.

Fort McHenry

Twenty-three *national memorials* help to recall important persons or events in American history. Often memorials are built *after* a person dies or in a different spot from where the event happened. The famous monuments in Washington, D.C., are national memorials. And in Bradenton, Florida, a national memorial honors Hernando de Soto, the Spanish explorer who landed here in 1539.

Our country's park service also protects many of America's famous battlegrounds. For example, Gettysburg, Pennsylvania, is a national military park. President Lincoln delivered his famous Gettysburg Address there in 1863, to dedicate the cemetery in which more than seven thousand soldiers were buried.

The Blue Ridge Mountains are part of the Appalachian Mountain chain that runs from Maine to Georgia.

Waterways and Land Preserves

Some of America's most beautiful bodies of water are also protected by the National Park Service. These places include eighteen *national recreation areas*, land around bodies of water created by dams. Other water areas protected by the park service include lakeshores, seashores, and rivers of special beauty.

As for land areas, designated *national parkways* are protected areas that run alongside beautiful stretches of highway. *National preserves* set aside areas rich in one or more natural resources, such as a special kind of wood or mineral. And *national scenic trails* are long-distance hiking trails, such as the 2,100-mile Appalachian National Scenic Trail that runs from Maine to Georgia.

Chronology

1492   Christopher Columbus sets sail from Spain.

1542   Juan Rodríguez Cabrillo is the first European to explore California.

1814   American troops defeat British forces at Fort McHenry, near Baltimore.

1848   Work begins on the Washington Monument. The first convention for women's rights is held.

1872   Yellowstone is designated as America's first national park.

1876   France gives the Statue of Liberty to the United States as a gift to mark America's 100th birthday.

1903   The Wright Brothers make the first successful airplane flight.

1914   Work begins on the Lincoln Memorial.

1923   Work begins on the Confederate Memorial.

1927   Work begins on Mount Rushmore.

1938   Work is started on the Jefferson Memorial.

1941   Japanese bomb Pearl Harbor, sinking *U.S.S. Arizona,* and killing over 1,000 of its crew.

1954   Marine Corps Memorial is dedicated.

1963   Construction begins on the Gateway Arch in St. Louis.

1982   Vietnam Veterans Memorial is dedicated in Washington, D.C.

1989   Civil Rights Memorial is built.

For Further Reading

Goetzmann, William, ed. *From Coronado to Escalante: The Explorers of the Spanish Southwest.* Bromall, PA: Chelsea House, 1990.

Miller, N. *The Lincoln Memorial.* Chicago: Childrens Press, 1990.

Miller, N. *The Statue of Liberty.* Chicago: Childrens Press, 1990.

Scott, David L. & Kay W. *Guide to the National Park Areas: Eastern States.* Chester, CT: The Globe Pequot Press, 1987.

Scott, David L. & Kay W. *Guide to the National Park Areas: Western States.* Chester, CT: The Globe Pequot Press, 1987.

Wright, D. *The Vietnam Veterans Memorial.* Chicago: Childrens Press, 1990.

Index

American Museum of Immigration, 35
Anasazi Indians, 31
Appalachian Mountains, 44
Appalachian National Scenic Trail, 45
Arlington National Cemetery, 15–19

Bartholdi, Frédéric Auguste, 35, 36
Black Hills, South Dakota, 12
Bloomer, Amelia Jenks, 39
Blue Ridge Mountains, 44
Borglum, Gutzon, 13, 38
Borglum, Lincoln, 13
Boston National Historical Park, 43
    Boston Tea Party, 43
    Old North Church, 43
    Old South Meeting House, 43
    U.S.S. Constitution, 43
Bradenton, Florida, 44

Cabrillo, Juan Rodríguez, 29, 30
Cabrillo National Monument, 29, 30
Capitol building, 7, 11
Carver, George Washington, 25
    National Monument, 25
Chaco Culture National Historical Park, 42
Cherry Blossom Festival, 11
Christopher Columbus Quincentennial Jubilee
    Commission, 30
Civil rights, fight for, 26
Civil Rights Memorial, 36, 37
Civil War, 9, 15, 25, 32, 38
Cliff Palace, 31
Close Encounters of the Third Kind, 43
Columbus, Christopher, 30
Columbus, Ohio, 30
Confederate Memorial Carving, 13, 38
Coronado, Francisco Vásquez de, 33
Coronado National Memorial, 33

Davis, Jefferson, 38
Death Valley National Monument, 5, 42
Declaration of Independence, 11, 23, 24
Democratic party, 27
Denali National Park and Preserve, 43
De Soto, Hernando, 44

Devils Tower, 43
De Weldon, Felix, 18

Ebenezer Baptist Church, 26
Eiffel, Alexandre Gustave, 36
Eiffel Tower, 36
Ellis Island immigration station, 35
Evans, Rudulph, 12
Everglades National Park, 43

Faulkner, Roy, 38
Fort McHenry, 43
Franklin, Benjamin, 5, 23
    National Memorial, 23, 24
French, Daniel Chester, 10

Gateway Arch, 32
Gettysburg Address (Lincoln's), 10, 44
Gila River Reservation, Arizona, 19
Grand Canyon, 41, 42
Great Smoky Mountains National Park, 42

Harper, Charles L., 26
Hayes, Corporal Ira, 19
Huachuca Mountains, 33
Hyde Park, New York, 27

Independence Hall, 24
Independence National Historical Park, 24
Iwo Jima, 17, 18

Jackson, Stonewall, 38
Jefferson Memorial, 5, 11
Jefferson National Expansion Memorial, 32
Jefferson, Thomas, 5, 11, 12, 32

Kennedy, John F., 42
Key, Francis Scott, 43
Kill Devil Hills, North Carolina, 24
King, Coretta Scott, 26
King, Jr., Martin Luther, 25, 26, 39
    Martin Luther King, Jr., Center for
        Nonviolent Social Change, 26
    Martin Luther King, Jr., National Historic
        Site, 25

47

Kitty Hawk, North Carolina, 24
Korean War, 16

Lazarus, Emma, 36
Lee, Robert E., 38
Liberty Bell, 24
Liberty Island, 34
Life magazine, 18
Lin, Maya, 21, 36
Lincoln, Abraham, 5, 9, 10, 12, 44
Lincoln Memorial, 4, 8, 9, 10, 11
Louisiana Purchase, 32

Marine Corps Memorial, 17, 18, 19
Massachusetts, 43
McClintock, Mary Ann, 39
Memphis, Tennessee, 21
Mesa Verde National Park, 31
Mississippi River, 33
Montgomery, Alabama, 36
Monticello, 11
Mott, Lucretia, 39
Mount McKinley, 43
Mount Rushmore, 12, 13, 38
Mount Suribachi, 17
Mount Vernon, Virginia, 41

National Mall, 7, 20
National Park Service, 5, 41, 44, 45
National Women's Hall of Fame, 39
New York City, 35
New York Harbor, 34
Niña, 30

Old Courthouse, 32
Old Faithful geyser, 42

Parthenon, the, 10
Pearl Harbor, Japanese bombing of, 19
Philadelphia, Pennsylvania, 23
Pinta, 30
Pueblo Indians, 33

Revere, Paul, 43
Revolutionary War, 15
Roosevelt, Eleanor, 5
    Eleanor Roosevelt National Historic Site,
    27
Roosevelt, Franklin D., 27

Roosevelt, Theodore, 12
Rosenthal, Joe, 18

Saarinen, Eero, 32
Saguaro National Monument, 43
San Diego, California, 29, 30
Santa Maria, 30
Scott, Dred, 32
Scruggs, Jan, 20
Seneca Falls, New York, 39
Seven Cities of Cíbola, 33
Shiloh National Military Park, 15
Southern Poverty Law Center, 37
Stanton, Elizabeth Cady, 39
Star-Spangled Banner, 43
Statue of Liberty National Monument, 29, 34,
    35
    facts about, 36
St. Louis, Missouri, 32
Stone Cottage, 27
Stone Mountain, Georgia, 13, 38

Tidal Basin, 11
Tomb of the Unknowns, 16, 17
Tuskegee Institute, 25

United Nations, 27
United States Constitution, 23, 24
U.S.S. Arizona Memorial, 19

Val-Kill Creek, 27
Valley Forge, Pennsylvania, 15
Vietnam Veterans Memorial, 7, 15, 20, 21, 36
Vietnam War, 16, 20

War of 1812, 43
Washington, Booker T., 25
Washington, D.C., 4, 5, 7, 15, 20, 36, 44
Washington, George, 4, 5, 7, 8, 12, 15, 41
Washington Monument, 5, 7, 8, 9, 11, 33
Wesleyan Methodist Chapel, 39
White House, 11
Women's Rights National Historic Park, 39
World War I, 16
World War II, 16, 18, 19
Wright Brothers (Wilbur and Orville), 24

Yellowstone National Park, 42
Yosemite National Park, 41